America:
American History for Children

Written and Illustrated by
Lori Kaiser

Visit Lori's website for other great books at:
www.lorikaiser.com

To follow Lori's current writings, visit:
www.kaiserbookblog.wordpress.com

Published by
Carpe Diem Publishers
17401 Betty Blvd.
Canyon, TX 79015
806-433-6321

www.carpediempublishers.com

© Copyright, 2010 by Carpe Diem Publishers. All Rights Reserved. No portion of this book may be reproduced, stored in a retrieval system, or transmitted, in any form or by any means, electronic, mechanical, photocopying, recording, or otherwise without prior written permission from publisher.
Printed in the United States of America
ISBN 978-0-9845761-1-1

To my husband Donnie,
who taught me how to dream.

By unanimous vote George Washington would lead.

At that time no one knew if the Republic would last.

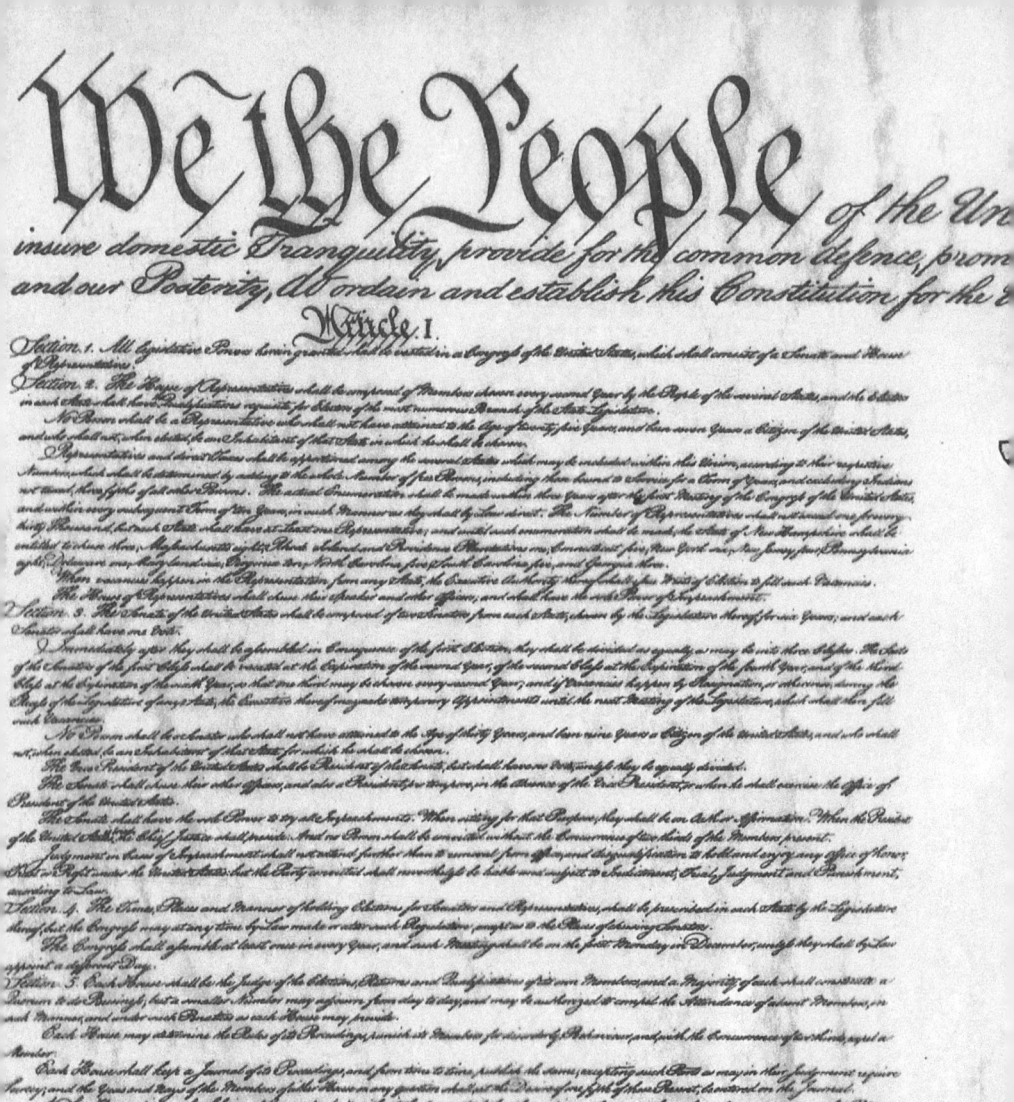

Our Constitution is important and must be preserved.

ONE NATION

Each president has to take a short oath

God has certainly blessed this "Land of the Free."

Preamble of the Constitution of the United States of America

We the People of the United States, in Order to form a more perfect Union, establish Justice, insure domestic Tranquility, provide for the common defence, promote the general Welfare, and secure the Blessings of Liberty to ourselves and our Posterity, do ordain and establish this Constitution for the United States of America.

Part of the Declaration of Independence

We hold these truths to be self-evident, that all men are created equal, that they are endowed by their Creator with certain unalienable Rights, that among these are Life, Liberty and the pursuit of Happiness.

Resources

National Geographic - The Making of America
    By: Historian Robert D. Johnston, PH.D.

A Grand Old Flag: A History of the United States Through its Flags
    By: Kevin Keim & Peter Keim

National Geographic - Our Country's Presidents
    By: Ann Bausam

Flags Pictured in Book

Flag dated 1876 - This flag was known as the Great Union and was flown during the early stages of the American Revolution. It was used to commemorate the Centennial and was flown over Independence Hall on July 4, 1876.

Flag dated 1791 - This fourteen star flag was never made official and is very rare. Vermont became the fourteenth state on March 4, 1791.

Footnotes

1 "Question with boldness" - Thomas Jefferson
2 "Speak without fear" - Thomas Jefferson

Definitons

Republic - A representative government ruled by law and recognizes the inalienable rights of the people. A Republic looks to the Constitution.

Democracy - A direct government ruled by the majority of the people and are only concerned with that group's wants or needs. A Democracy looks to the mob, and they rule.

www.ingramcontent.com/pod-product-compliance
Lightning Source LLC
Chambersburg PA
CBHW042046290426
44109CB00001B/49